HAVE YOU BEEN TO THE ALTAR LATELY?

Your Encounters Are a Result
of the Word of God and the Ministry of the
Holy Spirit

Kevin L. Zadai

HAVE YOU BEEN TO THE ALTAR LATELY?

HAVE YOU BEEN TO THE ALTAR LATELY?

Cover design: Virtually Possible Designs
Editing by Lisa Thompson at www.writebylisa.com
For more information about our school, go to www.warriornotesschool.com.
Reach us on the internet: www.Kevinzadai.com

ISBN 13 TP: 9798533569811

HAVE YOU BEEN TO THE ALTAR LATELY?

CONTENTS

HAVE YOU BEEN TO THE ALTAR LATELY?

Introduction

Some of the most intimate and memorable times of my life were the times I spent at an altar with God. An altar is a special meeting place where I commune with my Creator. I also met my Savior, Jesus Christ, there and fell in love with Him. At the altar, I made commitments through a covenant to walk before Him in the holy fire. Finally, the altar is a place where you bring everything you want to leave—sin, burdens, worry, fear, problems, and more—never to take them back again. In exchange, he gives you supernatural impartations and holy gifts to use in a mighty move of His Holy Spirit. At the altar, some things die, and other things receive life. It is time, my friend. Have you been to the altar lately?

Kevin L. Zadai
Founder and President of Warrior Notes and
Warrior Notes School of Ministry

HAVE YOU BEEN TO THE ALTAR LATELY?

Experiential Knowledge

1

They will act religious, but they will reject the
power that could make them godly.
Stay away from people like that!
—2 Timothy 3:5 NLT

Christianity must manifest for it to actually be valid, true Christianity. This means that others should be able to witness the effectiveness of our faith. Jesus was promoting the relationship He had with the Father. You could see this in His life and ministry as recorded in the Word of God. Remember, you gave your life to the Lord because you were aware that you needed a Savior through the Holy Spirit's revelation. Something occurred, and you had an experience.

HAVE YOU BEEN TO THE ALTAR LATELY?

You cannot take the experience out of salvation. I do not write my own doctrine based on my encounters, but my encounters are a result of the Word of God, the ministry of the Holy Spirit, and how that impacts me. It is transformative. It changes us so that we personally experience God.

But we have a problem. Many people are not experiencing God, so there is a disconnect between people and their Creator. The people that promote religion without experience are clouds without rain; they look legitimate, but they have no manifestation. So you can have a form of godliness; you can play the part, but you do not have the power.

"These false teachers are like dangerous hidden reefs at your love feasts, lying in wait to shipwreck the immature. They feast among you without reverence, having no shepherd but themselves. They are clouds with no rain, swept along by the winds. Like fruitless late-autumn trees—twice dead, barren, and plucked up by the roots!" (Jude 1:12 TPT).

When we gather together, wouldn't it be significant if one person got healed? We would be excited for the one, but we also have hope that we may be the next in line to receive. We do not give up because everyone did not get healed, and even if one person were changed or touched, it would be evidence that Jesus was among us. So you cannot minimize the power of that.

Jesus told me to be a self-feeder in the Word of God by studying and meditating on truth myself. At that time, I was not always receiving sound biblical teaching from the available avenues. I was frustrated with the lukewarm temperature of some messages; I would not receive anything at times! Yet I watched and listened to certain people with the touch of God on their lives, and when they spoke, they were talking from the other realm. As I listened, my heart warmed within me, and my spirit would light up. I would learn something. I would walk away a changed man from that time with an experience.

I did not have to go through all the activities of standing in line to be prayed for or getting a word from a minister. I received from God, and I took note of those people. I can listen to an old, crackling Kathryn Kuhlman tape and be touched by God. I can read one quote from John G. Lake, and I am transformed inside. Is there anyone like that today? Why can't we have someone like that today? Someone like Smith Wigglesworth. You can drop one of his books and read wherever it opens to, and you are amazed at how good it is. Well, like these saints of old, we should be able to hear from the Lord ourselves and then minister from the same Holy Spirit just as effectively to others around us.

HAVE YOU BEEN TO THE ALTAR LATELY?

Heavenly Flames of Fire

I will not stop testifying and sharing my experience about what the Word of God means to me because that connects me with the same God. That experiential knowledge drew me to the Lord. I want to tell you that an altar in heaven is on fire right now. Heaven is full of the glory and the holy fire of the Lord. The seraphim angels there are on fire.

We all have an angel assigned to us. My personal angel has seldom spoken to me since the day he introduced himself to me years ago. My wife and my pastor's mother at the time were there. He introduced himself once, and he is now in every service to help me. He seldom talks to me, and he doesn't have wings. He is on fire, smiling all the time, and I have never seen him sad. He is on fire because that is what he is, a minister of fire. He's been sent to serve those who will inherit salvation. "Who makes His angels spirits, His ministers a flame of fire" (Psalm 104:4). "And of the angels He says: 'Who makes His angels spirits and His ministers a flame of fire'" (Hebrews 1:7).

I could go my whole life and never tell you what I have experienced in the Spirit, but that does not mean the Spirit is not moving. But why do that? Why not let you know so that you can understand that when you are in a difficult situation, it isn't over yet? It is experiential knowledge. You have to have the Lord with you all the time, even when things don't go right.

When you do everything that you can do to stand and it all goes wrong, well, then you need someone to preach and teach and encourage you through that time. A process that takes time happens from when you received the Word of God, when it is established, and when it manifests. Time is involved in this process, but that is in this realm only.

In heaven, a fire that is never going out is on the altar at the throne of God right now. This fire on that altar was started by God, and you have been baptized in that same fire. However, we have to do certain things ourselves. If I take the *personal experience* out of Christianity, what do I have left? Cold religion.

Experiencing the Power from on High

If we cannot come and testify about what the Lord has done for us, then we have a religious system. We do not have Christianity. It is Christ with us, Immanuel. (See Isaiah 7:14.) The whole idea is this: God is interacting with man, not leaving him to fend for himself. It is not about being agnostic, where God initiates something and steps back, and you are on your own. That is what religion does. Religion leaves us to ourselves, but God is not like that. What would

7

you do if you had this happen to you and you saw that religion sends people to hell? Jesus had to deal with this when He spoke to the scribes and Pharisees in the book of Matthew. "Woe to you, scribes and Pharisees, hypocrites! For you travel land and sea to win one proselyte, and when he is won, you make him twice as much a son of hell as yourselves" (Matthew 23:15).

Jesus told this to the Pharisees who were part of the religious sect of His day. Today, religion spends so much money pushing their anti-biblical doctrine, and then they go after charismatic Christians. They try to make believers feel foolish, yet we have the power of God. We have the Holy Spirit given to us on the day of Pentecost. (See Acts 2:1–13.) Every Christian that is truly born again has that same power.

We see this manifestation in the baptism of the Holy Spirit, which is an added experience in the book of Acts. This experience was given to us to have power from heaven to be witnesses. We can be backward and not know how to handle ourselves in life, but the Spirit comes and super-intercedes for us and causes us to be bold and speak from the fire. I know whether someone is speaking from the holy fire. We need to learn how to speak from that place inside us where the Holy Spirit's fire resides because our spirit is ignited with the same fire that is on the altar of God.

HAVE YOU BEEN TO THE ALTAR LATELY?

When I think of you reading this, I am reminded that you are my family. You are a real person who loves God and loves me, but you are not reading this to hear from me. You are reading this to hear from the Lord. You want me to yield to the Holy Spirit so that you get a hot meal from heaven because you want that heavenly manna. Growing up, I longed for this supernatural manna, but as the days went by, I knew very few people with that touch from heaven through their voices. But now, I know there is a shortcut. You have to turn yourself in and come to the altar of God.

Some moms at home have children with more of a touch from God than some popular ministers. I have met them, and they have changed my life. Do you want to know why? Because they made comments inspired by the Holy Spirit and helped me walk on with God another day. I am not just doing ministry for myself but because I see a deficit out there, and this is the Lord's ministry. I am doing what I know will fill that deficit. I want to see people touched by God.

We cannot interpret everything in this life. We might never understand some things, but I want to be a master at what we can understand. I want to know what will hurt me and what will help me. What I don't know could hurt me. I want to know the truth. However, you have to be established and willing to receive the truth because you are responsible for it once you receive it. You will have to change and move with truth, and many people cannot do that past a certain point. It is time that we visit the altar of God.

Famine for God's Word

To compensate for not changing and moving with God, believers will engage in so-called Christian activities that are really just entertainment. They listen to a speaker and say, "Oh, that's cool, but, you know, so-and-so said this." They compare and criticize. Please do not let your experiential knowledge with God become entertainment instead of a life-changing experience.

My wife and I couldn't wait for powerful men and women of God to minister to us through the media or in church. We would prepare and wait for the service to begin. We wanted to be changed, to hear a fresh word from the throne of God. But ministry that does not come from spending time at the heavenly altar can stop transforming us so that we just let it become entertainment. It becomes a nice story to us, but did it change us? Unfortunately, we are getting to the place where there is a famine for the Word of God. (See Amos 8:11–12.) This is not the time for a famine because we need to hear from God more than ever.

I had been placing a demand on everyone else to minister to me, and then Jesus spoke to me about feeding myself. I was doing it in the right spirit because I was putting a demand on the gift that was in a person. At that time, I worked as a flight attendant, and some passengers were business people and Christians, and they often touched my life. More than one said, "You are a Christian, aren't you?"

I said, "Yes."

They replied, "You have the love of Jesus in your eyes, and I want to thank you. You were the best flight attendant I have ever had."

I also had witches and new-age passengers on flights, and they wanted to give me a tarot card reading and automatic writing. They said, "You're one of the chosen ones, and I can see the glow of the light on you. You've been enlightened."

I said, "No, I met Jesus."

They said, "I have this reading for you."

I told them, "No thanks. You tell your father that my Father wants to talk to him."

I am going to say something, and then I will never say it again. If you don't get it, I am sorry because I will not explain it. A spirit is out there, the new-age spirit, which is just witchcraft wrapped up nicely in wrapping paper and tied with a beautiful bow. The new-age doctrine is from hell, and it is just rewrapped. I don't know how else to say this, but that spirit influences some ministers, and they allow that false doctrine to come into their ranks. We must stay at a high temperature in the Spirit and keep the Word of God before us.

Raising the Heat

When Derek Prince came to a church to speak and minister, it didn't matter whether you thought someone was the holiest person in your church. They would start screaming out profanities because a devil was leaving them. That is what happened when Derek Prince showed up. I also witnessed this when Lester Sumrall came to speak at my church. I saw great people in our church start screaming and cursing him, and he was only talking about the offering. Well, you know, someone could get upset about the offering, but the member doesn't usually curse the speaker.

Ministers who understand their authority in Christ might be very controversial, but the thing is, I saw people act up and then be delivered of demons. The temperature had risen in those meetings because someone was walking in authority, and the demonic entities could not stay quiet in those people. Those people seemed fine until someone in authority showed up. Many church activities need to have a higher spiritual level so that people will experience freedom from these demonic spirits. It had to do with the fact that they had given themselves over to familiar spirits, and you could sense the change in them because it was different. It was the new-age influence.

A self-feeder of the Word who has been to the altar of God goes to church to give to others. It may be a word of encouragement or a prophetic word. It may be giving money. When I go to church, I make sure to carry extra cash to give to people in addition to what I bring for the offering. I pray and ask God to show me who I am supposed to give the money to, and I pray until I get a word for someone. I will have a picture of someone in my mind, and I get a word of encouragement for them. I go to church to give the word and give some money, and then I go home. If I never get a word or hear a nice sermon, I don't worry because I was fed in my prayer times alone with the Lord while reading the Bible. I have learned to be a self-feeder, and this is a shortcut. It is time to be transformed at the altar of our Lord.

PRAYER

Lord, I know that you are with me and desire to reveal yourself to me. Lead me according to your Word and manifest your goodness to me, in Jesus's name. Cause your ministry to flow out of me as I spend time at your holy altar! Amen!

What did the Holy Spirit reveal to you regarding this chapter?

_____

_____

_____

_____

_____

_____

_____

_____

_____

_____

_____

_____

_____

_____

_____

_____

_____

_____

_____

_____

_____

_____

_____

_____

HAVE YOU BEEN TO THE ALTAR LATELY?

Becoming a Carrier of the Fire

2

*Also I heard the voice of the Lord, saying
"Whom shall I send, And who will go for Us?"
Then I said, "Here am I! Send me."*
—Isaiah 6:8

When you go to the altar personally and catch on fire, you become an outflow. You become a carrier of that fire and the heavenly provision, and you are not needy anymore. Some of you think that the altar means death, but don't you agree that the altar can also be a memorial? It can be a place where you have met with God, and then you can return to that place, which will always be a memorial.

17

HAVE YOU BEEN TO THE ALTAR LATELY?

When we were in Israel, we went to Mount Carmel and stood right where Elijah defeated the prophets of Baal. (See 1 Kings 18:20–40.) I could see where the spring comes out and where Elijah would have gotten the water for the altar. You can still see the altar rocks that Elijah poured water on. In all the Israel tour, I felt God so strong in only three places, and one of them was on Mount Carmel. I felt the anointing of Elijah on that mountain, and it got on me, and I am changed because of that experience.

I also felt God's presence on the Mount of Olives. When we were there, I began to prophesy to our whole group as we all held hands. I said, "One day, He will come and split this mountain and come for us." The power of God hit us so strongly; it was a holy place.

My favorite place was Jesus's headquarters in Capernaum, where He lived and spoke in that very synagogue. I stood on the floor; everything is still there. I saw the foundation where Peter, his mother, and mother-in-law lived. It was His headquarters, and I could sense Jesus there.

It may surprise you, but like Elijah, one of my favorite places to meet with God and make an altar is where the witches make their sacrifices. It is their high place where they sacrifice animals. I go up to that high place that everyone is afraid of, so you won't find many ministers up there. But the power of God is so strong, I can hardly stand. Some memorials and places are dedicated to the occult, but what if your assignment is to take back a satanic altar that God wants to convert to His holy place? What if you are supposed to take back people's lives? Yes, we are supposed to reclaim people and places and take them back, and then *they* become a holy place. That is a warrior.

> Then one of the seraphim flew to me, having in his hand a live coal which he had taken with the tongs from the altar. And he touched my mouth with it, and said: "Behold, this has touched your lips; Your iniquity is taken away, and your sin purged." Also I heard the voice of the Lord, saying: "Whom shall I send, And who will go for Us?" Then I said, "Here am I! Send me." (Isaiah 6:6–8)

The same fire that came on the day of Pentecost originated from the throne of God and the holy altar. Isaiah encountered just the coal, and it cleansed him and cleansed a whole people. It changes you right now because you can receive an impartation by reading and hearing. The holy fire changes you because God is an all-consuming fire, and that fire touched Isaiah. "Since we are receiving our rights to an unshakeable kingdom we should be extremely thankful and offer God the purest worship that delights his heart as we lay

19

down our lives in absolute surrender, filled with awe. For our God is a holy, devouring fire!" (Hebrews 12:28–29).

The holy transference is not visible to the naked eye, yet it is in existence right now and wants to change all of us. If you do not believe something, it not only doesn't change you, but you will not to participate in it. You have to use the imaging ability that God gave you to let Him frame your perception of the Word of God from the text into an image.

The Power of Imaging

"And the Lord said, 'Indeed the people are one and they all have one language, and this is what they begin to do; now nothing that they propose to do will be withheld from them. Come, let Us go down and there confuse their language, that they may not understand one another's speech'" (Genesis 11:6–7).

To help you understand this concept of imaging, you can read what happened when they built the Tower of Babel. (See Genesis 11:1–9 AMPC.) Their hearts were set on evil, and God said that if He did not go down and confuse them, then they would be able to do anything they imagined. If your imagination isn't worth much, then why did God get off His throne and come down to stop a group of people from being able to image and communicate in agreement with one another? Why did He break up their plans? God said, "Now nothing that they propose to do will be withheld from them."

Let me explain something profound here. The secret to having great faith is in the definition, which was given to us in the book of Hebrews. "Now faith brings our hopes into reality and becomes the foundation needed to acquire the things we long for. It is all the evidence required to prove what is still unseen (Hebrews 11:1 TPT)."

So you can see that faith actually obtains evidence (image) that proves that we have what is unseen in the spirit realm. This requires us to see something that genuinely exists on the other side. When the Holy Spirit supernaturally gives us the reality of this, it becomes an imaged reality in us. We will not be denied when this process happens. If the evil people at Babel were capable of having everything imagined so that God Almighty had to stop them, how much more does that hold true now with us? We, as believers, have the truth of God and can imagine that powerful truth of the kingdom of heaven. Next, we implement that image in the earthly realm through the prayer of faith.

After the truth (image) is formed in us, the testimony of Jesus is all about verbalizing the truths by proclaiming them. "And I fell at his feet to worship him. But he said to me, 'See that you do not do that! I am your fellow servant, and of your brethren who have the testimony of Jesus. Worship God! For the testimony of Jesus is the spirit of prophecy'" (Revelation 19:10).

Paul emphasized the importance of prophecy in the public assembly so that the church assembly could be built up. This causes unity and agreement among the believers to bring forth the will and kingdom of God on earth. "I wish you all spoke with tongues, but even more that you prophesied; for he who prophesies is greater than he who speaks with tongues, unless indeed he interprets, that the church may receive edification" (1 Corinthians 14:5).

The Word of God has to come off the page and be imaged. What we believe must be applicable to our daily lives. The Bible talks about those people who have a form of godliness but deny the power thereof. They will not promote experiential knowledge and forbid you to have a manifestation of the biblical text.

For instance, we talk about prophecy and about interpreting your tongues, which is equal to prophecy. However, when you actually pray in other tongues and interpret it, or prophesy, you are fulfilling Scripture. But some churches do not believe that this is for today. Paul said to pray that you prophesy because that will help everyone in a congregation.

HAVE YOU BEEN TO THE ALTAR LATELY?

It is time to worship at the altar and then testify of Jesus everywhere you go.

Prophecy: A Call from the Altar

"And I fell at his feet to worship him. But he said to me, 'See that you do not do that! I am your fellow servant, and of your brethren who have the testimony of Jesus. Worship God! For the testimony of Jesus is the spirit of prophecy'" (Revelation 19:10).

The book of Revelation says here that the spirit of prophecy is the testimony of Jesus. When I am around the right crowd of believers, sitting at a restaurant table, the spirit of prophecy will come upon me. That spirit of prophecy is a literal flame or a call from the altar of God. I get ignited inside because I am about to prophesy. All of a sudden, I start to talk about the Lord and what His intention is. I am just talking across the table to someone, but the power is so strong, and suddenly everyone in the restaurant stops talking. I am talking to the table, but my words go into the room.

We have seen this happen so many times. Suddenly, the other diners' spirits pick up that something from the other realm is being said, and the room goes silent. Even though 80 percent of them may be unsaved and going to hell, their spirits pick up that something is being said from the heavenly realm. Everyone gets quiet, and if you went around the room, no one could explain why they stopped talking because they wouldn't know why. As soon as I am done testifying about the Lord or saying something from that other realm, everyone will pick up their conversations and start talking again.

When I listen to a person ministering, I desire to hear them speak from the heavenly realm. We do not desire to hear someone simply talk *about* God but someone to talk *for* God. Is that asking too much? You can compare this to the meat by-product in a can that no one can even identify versus a nice juicy steak. You and I cannot live off substandard food. After a while, your bad diet will show up in your life. I desire fellow Christians speaking by the Spirit to give us the Word of God because they have spent time at the altar and are not mysterious and obscure. God was mysterious until Jesus came, but when Jesus came, our heavenly Father took the mystery out of it because He gave us the Holy Spirit. "For 'who has known the mind of the Lord that he may instruct Him?' But we have the mind of Christ" (1 Corinthians 2:16).

When you read 1 Corinthians 2, the passage reveals that we now have the mind of Christ. We have the same Spirit that reveals God to us, and now we know God. God will be more than we will ever know, but the Spirit of God takes the mystery out of God by revealing Him to us.

HAVE YOU BEEN TO THE ALTAR LATELY?

There Are No Lukewarm Christians

Believers present themselves to God on a holy altar. But the altar is not a place to die physically. You meet God there and *die to your own selfish desires.* You are to be a living sacrifice.

"And so, dear brothers and sisters, I plead with you to give your bodies to God because of all he has done for you. Let them be a living and holy sacrifice—the kind he will find acceptable. This is truly the way to worship him. Don't copy the behavior and customs of this world, but let God transform you into a new person by changing the way you think. Then you will learn to know God's will for you, which is good and pleasing and perfect" (Romans 12:1–2).

Sometimes the altar is so that you can receive something from the heavenly realm and bring it into the physical realm by faith.

We will even see a housewife with little ones move into the deep things of God because she has been touched by Him. She intercedes for breakthrough for people to be the next prayer warrior and minister. Most of us are done with what is classified as "Christian" but is just nice talk. At what point are we transformed so that we see our prayers answered in a supernatural way?

HAVE YOU BEEN TO THE ALTAR LATELY?

I have been talking about the heavenly shortcut called *altar time*, and religious people try to make it complicated and exhausting. I said "shortcut" because Jesus paved the way for us so we just follow Him into the holy of holies. Jude talks about "clouds without rain," which are people who have a form of godliness without the power of the Holy Spirit present. These religious people are the goats that Jesus was referring to in the parables of separation, the separation that is occurring right now. Jesus came to seek and save those who are lost (lost sheep). (See Luke 19:10.) Once He finds you, you are not lost anymore, and then He baptizes you, and then you are on fire. The heavenly Father never wants to encounter a lukewarm Christian. "But since you are like lukewarm water, neither hot nor cold, I will spit you out of my mouth!" (Revelation 3:16 NLT).

Jesus clearly desires you to be either hot or cold, and because you are neither, He will spit you out of His mouth. All those churches that He was talking about were in northern Turkey. Those seven churches in the book of Revelation are all gone now. Half of them are now mosques, and the others are just rubble. So guess who was right? Jesus, of course.

PRAYER

Thank you, Lord, that I am not lukewarm and that I please you. Keep me hot on your holy altar of fire. Amen.

What did the Holy Spirit reveal to you regarding this chapter?

_____

_____

_____

_____

_____

_____

_____

_____

_____

_____

_____

_____

_____

_____

_____

_____

_____

_____

_____

_____

_____

_____

Hearing the Spirit at the Altar

3

*Anyone with ears to hear must listen
to the Spirit and understand
what he is saying to the churches.*
—Revelation 2:29 NLT

I have to talk about hearing what the Spirit is saying, which is experiential knowledge. I want everyone to receive profound revelation from the Spirit of God. Let the Holy Spirit supernaturally counsel you by giving you a reality of the truth from the Scripture, an encounter with Him. Jesus said that if you have ears to hear, you must hear what the

Spirit is saying. (See Revelation 3:22.) Obviously, the seven churches in the book of Revelation didn't hear or obey. Does that have to be the way it is with us? It has to do with this special altar and a memorial. We need to return to this holy place and have a supernatural encounter.

Abraham had an experience and encountered God at Bethel, building an altar there. (See Genesis 12:7–8.) Abraham built that altar, and because he was the father of us all, you would think that we would follow his example and that the next generation would honor it as well. Isaac, Abraham's son, went through there, and we see that God was with Isaac. (See Genesis 26:2–26.) So the transference went from Abraham, the patriarch, to Isaac.

However, when it reached the third generation, Jacob (Isaac's son), we start to see problems. Right from the start, from Jacob's birth, a lot of manipulation was going on. (See Genesis 25:22–28.) Jacob then became a manipulator and was manipulated. When Jacob was grown, he had to deal with Laban, his father-in-law. (See Genesis 31.) Throughout Jacob's whole life, he dealt with infighting and manipulation, but God was still with him.

The covenant that God made with Abraham and Isaac (the birthright) was passed down to Jacob. The covenant with God was still in effect, but was Jacob cooperating? He was not operating in the mantle of his grandfather or his father. The third generation started to fall away. You can see the regression, which then led to lukewarmness toward God, just like what happened in the new covenant. (See Revelation 3:16.)

It is time to go to the holy altar of God in prayer. The altar full of fire in heaven can change your temperature if you allow it to overtake you, but if you do not, you will be lukewarm. However, if you hang out with lukewarm people, you will feel fine, and they will feel comfortable around you. I notice that I am excluded from certain activities because people think that if they get around me, I will want to talk about God. Well, maybe that is what they need to do. I might show up anyway to make them take their medicine, which is the coal from the altar of God.

Establishing the Plumb Line

A lot of people don't know they are lukewarm until they experience *truth* from the Word of God, hot from the heavenly realm. Jeremiah the prophet showed the people a plumb line. Everyone called something that was crooked straight until Jeremiah showed up with the real plumb line from heaven, the Word of the Lord. (See Jeremiah 1:4–19.) When God called Jeremiah, he thought he was too young and he could not speak. But he held up the standard that God had

31

called him to, which affected so many people around him in Israel.

Think about what it would look like if this happened today. If Jeremiah or Elijah came back from the dead and became our president, you would not like them unless you were lined up with what God had already established as the righteousness that reigns from heaven. The government was formed to protect and serve you. They are being paid to represent us, protect us, and serve us, but not to control us. I am quoting the Constitution here: "We, the people" not "we, the government." Society has changed, and this is the lukewarm atmosphere we are living in now.

Would you be comfortable if Jesus told you the truth? Would you like everything He said? The chances of this happening in every church are low. Based on Scriptures, religious leaders and some people did not like everything Jesus said.

In one day, during Jesus's ministry, almost everyone left Him. Remember when He said, "Whoever eats My flesh and drinks My blood has eternal life, and I will raise him up at the last day." (See John 6:54–70.) After Jesus said this, many of His disciples left Him. Then Jesus turned to the twelve and said, "Do you also want to go away?"

HAVE YOU BEEN TO THE ALTAR LATELY?

Simon Peter answered, "Lord, to whom shall we go? You have the words of eternal life. Also we have come to believe that you are the Christ, the Son of the living God." So there is a cost to following Jesus.

If you want absolute truth, then a plumb line will tell you if you are off. A group of people or a nation can become out of alignment, and when Jesus comes to judge the world, it won't be pretty. A sword is coming out of His mouth. (See Revelation 19:15.) I have been released to tell you an experience I had in my bedroom in Seattle, Washington, when I was in disobedience. I woke up, and Jesus was standing at the foot of my bed. I could see by the look on His face that something was wrong and I was in trouble. I looked at Him, and He said, "I am the door."

I said, "Yes, you said that in John."

Jesus pointed at me and said, "You don't understand. You don't go anywhere on this earth unless it is through Me. Do you understand now?" He was stern about this subject and turned around and walked out without even saying goodbye.

I had accepted my first invitation to speak without asking Him. When I was in Bible school, I was told that you should never turn down an invitation when you first start in ministry because you are not established yet. I had not checked in with the Holy Spirit about this, and Jesus didn't like that. Jesus gave me access to the earth, but it was through Him, and He was hurt that I had not done it correctly. You are *sent* not *went*, and Jesus wanted me to clearly understand that as I started the ministry that He had given me. If Jesus doesn't send me, I don't go.

The Sword of Discipline

When Jesus appeared to me another time, I woke up, and He was standing there. He said, "Don't find yourself on the wrong side of Me." What was going on that He would say this to me? I was getting too comfortable and becoming lukewarm. I was getting kind of cozy, sipping my tea with Jesus, so to speak. I was hanging out with Jesus, and I got too casual.

Some days, during His ministry, Jesus thinned out the crowd by speaking hard-to-accept sayings. He explained something to me about this. He said, "My sword is a two-edged sword with two sides. One side is to cut you, and one is to cut your enemy." That sword of the Spirit is so sharp that it can divide; it cuts between your soul and your spirit. That is hard to discern because you don't know if that is your voice or God's voice. But the Word of God can go in there and do surgery. "For the word of God is living and powerful, and sharper than any two-edged sword, piercing even to the division of soul and spirit, and of joints and marrow, and is a discerner of the thoughts and intents of the heart" (Hebrews 4:12).

Jesus told me that sword is to discipline me, not to hurt me or to kill me, but to show me what is of me and what is of Him. I am not to find myself on the wrong side of Him during this process. In other words, I am never to find myself working against Him, thinking I am accomplishing the Father's will or doing Him a favor.

I make sure I watch my words. You do not use your tongue against God's people because we cannot speak against our own. It is a sharp sword, a sharp knife, and cannot be used to cut down one of the sheep.

There are sheep, and there are goats. You do not have any obligation to a goat because Jesus didn't. He had no obligation to the tares, just the wheat, and He had no obligation to the five unwise virgins. The five wise virgins were told *not* to help the unwise ones. (See Matthew 25:1–13 NIV.) When the foolish virgins asked the wise for their oil, the wise answered, "No, we don't have enough for all of us. Go to a shop and buy some for yourselves." Most people would say that is a lack of love and they were not walking in love. But it was too late when they went to get their oil, and the bridegroom came and left without them. They were all virgins, all ten of them, but only the five wise ones went with the bridegroom. You do not want to find yourself on the side, left behind.

Remembering the Altar

The altar of God is a genuine shortcut, so turn yourself in now. I encourage you to repent daily and become a self-feeder on the Word of God and then go to the shortcut, which is the altar. Jacob was the third generation that fell away, which is what we are encountering with right now in the church. We are suffering because we have a good report about God's plans. I am prophesying God's heart for this nation. As Christians, we have to go to the altar, and we get our standard from there. Then we stand, no matter what happens. Whatever happens, the altar is still hot, and we should go there. Unfortunately, Jacob did not, and what we had here was a failure to communicate. We have a problem because the standard of truth is still the same in heaven, but we have to deal with this physical realm not measuring up to what is needed in the situation down here.

What do we do? We don't fall away, and we don't bend or cool down, but we go to war in prayer. The same thing happened with Jacob, and he had to work his way out of his dilemma with the Lord. It is kind of sad, isn't it? But he had to have a name change and become Israel before he could cross the Jordan River into the promised land. (See Genesis 35:1–15.) He had to have a wrestling match with God. Do not find yourself on the wrong side of God because He will win. Jacob kept pushing away his altar, but in the end, he found it by default.

If you talked to Abraham, he would remember the altar he built, and then Isaac would remember the altar that his father built because Isaac went to Bethel as well. But isn't it interesting how Jacob was running, got tired, and accidentally, but by God's secret purpose, found himself in Bethel for a night? He fell asleep on one of the rocks that was probably part of the altar that Abraham built and had a dream about a ladder; he saw angels going up and down on it. (See Genesis 28:12–22.)

When Jacob woke up in Bethel in his lukewarm state, he said, "Surely the Lord is in this place, and I did not know it." Jesus told me that Jacob should have known it because of his heritage with his family roots. He should have known about the altar at Bethel. He should have honored the heritage he had in Abraham. The third generation after the altar experience of Abraham had problems. The understanding of their covenant with God and their spiritual vision faded. The Bible talks about this principle. It works for blessings and curses because there are curses to the third and fourth generation. (See Exodus 20:5.)

HAVE YOU BEEN TO THE ALTAR LATELY?

I have to bring up our culture because we do not respect our forefathers anymore, if you notice. They are even trying to get rid of the statues of our forefathers. They are destroying statues of people that actually stood up for them. It is where we are at, and in a generation, we are lost. We don't have the foundation of why we are here, what we believe in, or what we stand for. And because of that, we cannot discern that our government has become our boss who tells us what we can see and hear. Why do people who tell the truth disappear from YouTube and lose their credentials? "Righteousness and justice are the foundation of Your throne; mercy and truth go before Your face. Blessed are the people who know the joyful sound! They walk, O Lord, in the light of Your countenance" (Psalm 89:14–15).

At what point do we go to the altar and find the absolute truth of God and His throne? God has established His throne, and the foundation of His throne is righteousness and justice, and truth and faithfulness surround Him. God's angels are part of His entourage, but they also enforce His faithfulness, and they are assigned to help us. Do not forfeit the angelic or the gifts of the Holy Spirit in these last days by growing lukewarm. We cannot allow a temperature decrease, especially now when it looks like everything is being stolen from us. It is not the time to revise your theology. You cannot revise the layers in God's throne. (See Psalm 89.)

HAVE YOU BEEN TO THE ALTAR LATELY?

You cannot let anyone who is in the false new-age theology or someone who falsely calls themselves prophetic to shift you into forfeiting your covenant promises. You base what people say on the Word of God and if they are speaking from the Holy Spirit fire from the altar. The testimony of Jesus is the spirit of prophecy. (See Revelation19:10.) Does it shift the spiritual temperature in the room or in your life? Does it make unsaved people in a restaurant stop talking and listen? At what point do we require an experience in our life and not just head knowledge? There must be a manifestation of your faith because God is faithful.

PRAYER

Thank you, Lord, that I have ears to hear what the Spirit is saying in this hour. And I commit to go to the altar and find the absolute truth of God and His throne Amen.

What did the Holy Spirit reveal to you regarding this chapter?

_____

_____

_____

_____

_____

_____

_____

_____

_____

_____

_____

_____

_____

_____

_____

_____

_____

_____

_____

_____

_____

_____

_____

_____

HAVE YOU BEEN TO THE ALTAR LATELY?

The Kingdom Advancing through You

4

And as you go, preach, saying, "The kingdom of heaven is at hand." Heal the sick, cleanse the lepers, raise the dead, cast out demons. Freely you have received, freely give.
—Matthew 10:7–8

John the Baptist said that he was baptizing with water, but one was coming who would baptize you with the Holy Spirit and with fire. (See Matthew 3:11.) So everywhere Jesus went, He was manifesting the Father God, and the kingdom of God was advancing through Him. We think of Jesus as healing the sick and casting out devils. What was really happening was the kingdom was behind Him and was pushing out through Him.

Jesus never asked the demons to talk. He just cast them out and let the kingdom of God manifest. Is the kingdom advancing through you? At what point do we just go to the altar and take what is real and bring it back? At what point do we realize that when the kingdom is advancing, it is coming out through us, and it will affect everything and everyone around us?

Jesus was just going about doing good and healing everyone that was oppressed of the devil (Acts 10:38). He was representing the kingdom, and the kingdom was working through Him, but something was going on in the environment, and the devils were crying out. If you notice, they were crying out before Jesus even got to them. (See Matthew 8:1–32). They had already started acting up! The demons were already starting to negotiate, not wanting to be sent out of the area. Jesus had not even said anything or addressed them yet. "And suddenly they cried out, saying, 'What have we to do with You, Jesus, You Son of God? Have You come here to torment us before the time?' Now a good way off from them there was a herd of many swine feeding. So the demons begged Him, saying, 'If You cast us

44

out, permit us to go away into the herd of swine'" (Matthew 28:29–31).

The demons were negotiating their position because they did not want to leave their place. They had been in that area for years, decades, even for centuries, and they had built a matrix of how they dealt with people. They had their victims, which may even be you if you do not learn to escape. They target bloodlines, so they do not want to be sent out of the area, and they are there to enforce curses.

If they ask you not to send them out of the area, you say, "Thanks for letting me know what you don't want because that is exactly what I will do." They also asked not to be tormented before their time. "Thank you for letting me know that too." You start talking about the blood of Jesus, and they will be tormented and start to scream. You do whatever they tell you not to do.

The Kingdom Is Coming

The kingdom hit them before Jesus got there, and before you get there, the kingdom is coming. The dominion of God is working outwardly. People are already feeling the shift in the atmosphere so that when you speak, it is all set up to start the deliverance. The yoke-breaking power starts working so that blind eyes open and people see. You can deliver the

45

HAVE YOU BEEN TO THE ALTAR LATELY?

Word of the Lord in the marketplace. People will be struck with this power. They are not even saved yet, but they are about to be.

They could not resist the absolute truth of what Jesus was saying. But you have to have something from the heavenly realm, which is the realm of absolute truth. You have to allow your imagination to "image" the Word of God. There is power in agreement, even if people agree on something false. God said that He could not stop fallen men in Babylon from doing the evil they imagined unless He came down and confused and separated them. This is exactly what occurred at the Tower of Babel. God had to separate the continents and the languages to stop them, or they would have succeeded in their evil. (See Genesis 11:8–9.)

But God reversed that through the baptism of the Holy Spirit, which happened on the day of Pentecost. As I mentioned earlier, the "clouds without rain" people have a form of godliness but deny the power thereof. They fight against the validity of Pentecost for today.

> These false teachers are like dangerous hidden reefs at your love feasts, lying in wait to shipwreck the immature. They feast among you without reverence, having no shepherd but themselves. They are clouds with no rain,

swept along by the winds. Like fruitless late-autumn trees—twice dead, barren, and plucked up by the roots! They are wild waves of the sea, flinging out the foam of their shame and disgrace. They are misleading like wandering stars, for whom the complete darkness of eternal gloom has been reserved. (Jude 1:12–13)

The devil does not want the kingdom of our God to advance any further. These people say that Pentecost died with the cessation of the apostles. These people are called cessationists, and they believe that when the apostles died, the movement of the Holy Spirit was stopped. However, the same Holy Spirit is still inside us, and He hasn't changed. No one has the authority to say that it has all ended because it's not in Scripture unless you manipulate a couple of verses that talk about when we reach perfection. Only I have not met any perfect people yet, so we are not there. "And we know that all things work together for good to those who love God, to those who are the called according to His purpose" (Romans 8:28).

Jacob should have discerned that he was at Bethel, and he should have known that an altar was there, which was his power. That was his place to meet with God. Instead of that, he experienced a wrestling and a name change, and he limped the rest of his life. (See Genesis 32:22–32). That was not God's perfect will. It looked like it because all things work for good to those who love God and who are called according to His purpose. Jacob should have had a handoff from Isaac and Abraham.

It's Time for a Change

All the angels that have been assigned to you are standing beside you, and they know that you have read this. They know now that you must take this and apply it to your life where the rubber meets the road, as the saying goes. You can watch the videos on how to do something, but there will come a point when you have to do it yourself. I do not mind holding your hand while you do it, but we all must do it.

I know what the problem is, but I don't know how to tell people nicely. We have overemphasized the role of church leaders in the five-fold ministry and depended on them too much, just like we put too much emphasis on and depend on our government and its role. If something goes wrong, we don't go to church to get our provision because we expect the government to give us our handout. We do the same when we depend on the five-fold ministry of the church. We depend on the apostle, prophet, pastor, teacher, and evangelist and neglect our own responsibility to develop as believers.

HAVE YOU BEEN TO THE ALTAR LATELY?

The church should be the most prosperous and influential organization on the earth because everyone should be involved. The government should be coming to us to receive prayer for all the leaders, having hands laid on them. We should be the most powerful institution on the earth because we are, according to Jesus. The gates of hell cannot prevail against the church!

Why is the enemy bulldozing over the church and then turning around and backing up over us two or three times? I can almost hear some Christians saying, "Thank you. I think you missed a spot." I get the whole servant mentality and turning the other cheek. However, when it comes to dealing with the enemy, at one point, every knee will bow and every tongue confess that Jesus is Lord. (See Philippians 2:10–11.) There will be so many people cast into hell because they did not discern their day of visitation when God gave us His Son, Jesus. We need to go to the holy altar and lay our life down for Him. Submission to the holy altar fire will bring a great victory over our enemy. "Therefore submit to God. Resist the devil and he will flee from you" (James 4:7).

I would rather Christians submit at the altar and be hot. I desire to belong to a group of on-fire people who know how to go to the altar, take the fire within them, let it change them, and then change their environment. I am not going to lay down and let someone keep rolling back and forth over me.

HAVE YOU BEEN TO THE ALTAR LATELY?

I am done with this wrong attitude concerning God's will so that people say, "Whatever may come, let it be." We have authority to stop the enemy in Jesus's name when we submit our lives to Him at the holy altar.

I was told that evangelist Charles Finney worked hard to get through law school. When he finally got a law practice, then God told him to quit.[1] He gave up his law practice, and he went into the woods where he paced between two trees, praying. The price for revival is high because Charles had quit his job and had no income. He was similar to John G. Lake, a very wealthy businessman that the time, who gave up everything and prayed for people who had a contagious disease called the plague.

We need these types of healing evangelists now. I am only saying that because Jesus wants to heal everyone. He wants me to pray for people every week, whether in person, at conferences, or online. He wants to manifest His ministry through the church during this time. Once, I turned my cameras on every weekend and went live with thirteen Spirit Schools in a row, and I told the devil that I would keep doing

---

[1] "Charles Finney: Father of American Revivalism," *Christianity Today*, accessed June 11, 2021, https://www.christianitytoday.com/history/people/evangelistsandapologists/charles-finney.html.

it until he backed off. Now, here we are, four times the size that our ministry was then.

John G. Lake gave millions away and went to battle a foul disease that nearly killed him. He was transformed by the truth and hated that sickness so much that he left everything to destroy it. Charles Finney found himself going to God, arguing his case like a lawyer. Does that sound familiar? Abraham did the same in his yard because his nephew Lot was in Sodom and Gomorrah when God's angels came to destroy it. Abraham started wheeling and dealing to save the life of Lot. (See Genesis 18:22–33.) The price was high because he was about to lose his nephew.

What about Moses? Moses pleaded with God not to kill all the Israelites when they made their golden idols in the desert. (See Exodus 32:1–14.) His argument for not doing it was that all Egypt would think that God brought them out of Egypt to kill them. God told Moses that He would make a great nation out of him only, and Moses asked God not to do it. He asked God to remember His covenant with Abraham, Isaac, and Jacob, and God relented. He told God that if He did not go with them, they would not go. (See Exodus 33:15.)

HAVE YOU BEEN TO THE ALTAR LATELY?

Just One Touch

"And shall God not avenge His own elect who cry out day and night to Him, though He bears long with them? I tell you that He will avenge them speedily. Nevertheless, when the Son of Man comes, will He really find faith on the earth?" (Luke 18:7–8).

The same Holy Spirit is now upon the church. People are falling away and backsliding, but the Word warns us about a great falling away in these last days. Jesus asked, "When I return, will I find faith on the earth?" (See Luke 18:8.)

Take that one coal that touched Isaiah's lips, which is a couple of thousand years old now. (See Isaiah 6:6–7.) It changed a man, a nation, and history, and it changed us.

Imagine what would happen if you took that one coal that has already been used, and it touched you right now. I wait every second of every day for that to happen, for us to all be on the floor, crying out to God. I know what will happen, and it can happen right now. All that has to change is that the used coal has to touch you, and you will have more faith than you could get in a thousand years by meditating on the Word of God because it is a gift. Faith can be given to you as a special gift, a gift of faith.

HAVE YOU BEEN TO THE ALTAR LATELY?

It could be that easy. All of a sudden, you realize that you have been striving your whole life and all you needed was one touch, and it was all resolved. You won't remember what you were worried about, and you will forget about all your problems as you will be lying on the floor. It is called revival, but it is more than revival because you are not dead. It is called transformation because something supernatural from the other realm has touched you.

The stories and experiences of what I saw in heaven and the truth of the Word of God are so that you can grab hold of the experiential knowledge. I am getting you used to that because your moment is coming. Your time at the altar is here. Finney is hanging over the rails of heaven, shouting at you right now to listen. Smith Wigglesworth, John G. Lake, Steve Hill, David Wilkerson—you name them all—are shouting, "You can do this! You are going to experience things that we never did."

Many of those people prophesied that in God's last move, everyone would walk out healed. No one sick would be left in the building, and everyone would be healed just like that. The ministers that I trust, like Smith Wigglesworth and Kathryn Kuhlman, all prophesied this.

PRAYER

Lord, all of a sudden, we realize that our whole lives, we have been striving. All we needed was one touch to resolve all these matters. We won't remember what we were worried about. We will forget about all our problems. It is called transformation because something supernatural from your realm, Father, has touched us. Thank you, Jesus. Amen.

What did the Holy Spirit reveal to you regarding this chapter?

_____

_____

_____

_____

_____

_____

_____

_____

_____

_____

_____

_____

_____

_____

_____

_____

_____

_____

_____

_____

_____

_____

_____

_____

HAVE YOU BEEN TO THE ALTAR LATELY?

God's Recompense

5

Beloved, do not avenge yourselves, but rather
give place to wrath; for it is written "Vengeance
is Mine, I will repay," says the Lord.
—Romans 12:19

I have had the spiritual lightnings of God—blue lightning—hit me. I did not know that John G. Lake had a sermon about the lightnings of God, and he lived a long time before me. Recently a pastor said to me, "The Lord is telling me to give you something that I was told I could only give to one person. A relative of John G. Lake gave me these unpublished sermons, and I am supposed to give them to you."

I gave these sermons to a producer who works in Christian programming. He read one paragraph, and the power of God hit him. I cannot read them yet because I am writing right now, and I do not want the sermons to bleed over into what I am writing, but that is how powerful they are. Everyone will want to read these, and I am honored that God has trusted me with them.

When I was at Rhema Bible College, I could not afford to buy tapes, and if I did, I would have to work extra to afford them. I was working three jobs, but when gas went from 99 cents to $1.03 a gallon, I was in the red for the month over that four-cent price increase. I was always in a negative cash flow. I worked as a concierge at a five-star hotel, and I was thankful whenever I found quarters lying around.

If I could get enough money together, I could buy a cassette of brother Hagin (or whoever was teaching us) teaching my class at Rhema. I couldn't afford to buy my class tapes either, but I finally gathered enough money together and bought a whole set. It cost me around twenty-five dollars, and I gave them the money.

At that exact time, my grandma decided she would pay for my flight home, but I had to fly on a certain day, and I could not pick up my tapes. They told me that I would have to forfeit the tapes because I did not pick them up on time. I never got the tapes that I paid for because of the rules.

I visited the altar and committed this all to the Lord so that He could make it all right.

A couple of months after the first pastor gave me John G. Lake's sermons, another pastor said to me, "A very close relative of brother Hagin said that I could give this to one minister of my choosing. It is all of brother Hagin's sermons and all the classes at Rhema. I can pick one person, and you are that person." I now have all the classes. God was faithful to get them all to me.

I Want Payback

Where do you feel you have been in a deficit? Don't you think a visit to the altar will fix this? Don't you think that recompense will be severe? Once, someone stole my car. We were going to church, and it was gone from our parking spot. There were only a few models of this car made, and it was a collector's item. I had bought it with my own money before I was in the ministry, and the devil stole it.

59

HAVE YOU BEEN TO THE ALTAR LATELY?

My wife and I did not start crying. Instead, we called someone and had them pick us up for church. Afterward, we waited for the police because we had to fill out the police report. Just before we called the police, we agreed in prayer that not only would we get our car back, but the thieves would be caught and we would receive recompense. The matter would not just go to court, but we would receive recompense. Not many Christians go that far because they are so meek and mild, but I wanted payback.

"'I will take revenge; I will pay them back,' says the Lord" (Romans 12:19 NLT). Make room for the Lord, and stand back because it is not going to be pretty. It will be a light show because recompense is coming to you. It is not enough that the enemy is found out. He has to pay back what he stole as recompense. This is just as biblical as being caught.

When the police came, we filled out the report, and they said that the drug cartels ordered this car and gang members stole them to fulfill the order. They came across the border, looking for this car, and they had watched me for a long time. They knew that I had it. I told the officer, "I know we'll get it back," but he did not think so. I asked him, "What could I have done to prevent it?"

He said, "Well, we have found only one thing that works. Sleep in your car. But if they want your car, they will get it."

HAVE YOU BEEN TO THE ALTAR LATELY?

Three weeks later, we got a call to come down to the station and pick up our car. They had to tell us a story. One of the officers was running plates at 2:00 a.m. and came across a 7-Eleven, where he found my car backed into a spot in the front. Normally, if you see a car backed into a 7-Eleven at 2:00 a.m., a robbery or another crime is probably about to happen there.

Since the officer could not see the plate to run it, he got out of his car. The person in my car tried to start it to get away, and the kill switch ignited, which I had installed and which should have stopped them from the beginning. The problem was the kill switch was cut, but it worked when they tried to get away and locked them in the car with the alarm going off. So they got him. The officer said, "There is not a scratch on your car except for one thing. They cut the alarm system the first night they stole the car."

There was no way that the kill switch or the alarm could have worked because all the wires were cut, and they had pictures. Not only that, but are you ready for this? They put it on the tow truck to take it to the impound, but the alarm wouldn't turn off, even though the wires were cut. So they disconnected the battery, and the alarm kept going off the whole way to the impound. They could not get it to turn off. They even had pictures of the battery disconnected.

61

HAVE YOU BEEN TO THE ALTAR LATELY?

All the officers were blown away by this, but it didn't blow us away because of the covenant we have with our God and the prayer that we prayed. That thief made payments for years for that car. The restitution that they had to pay was more than what the car was worth. The judge ordered the car to be repainted any color we wanted, and as part of restitution, everything had to be redone to make it as though it were brand new. We received all that and the payment every month. When everything was paid for, we sold the car and made a lot of money off the whole thing. That is recompense, and that is restoration!

Engage with Heaven

After telling you this, you cannot exclude yourself because I am no different from you. What have you had stolen? *You need to visit the altar.* How long has it been since you have been to the altar? I bet if you laid down on the floor and fell asleep right now, there would be a ladder with angels going up and down on it, and you would be in Bethel, but you wouldn't even know it.

Right now, your angels are standing beside you, waiting for your call to engage them because it is true. You just need to imagine it because it is true. You cannot see your angels, but they are still real. God said this about the Babylonians:

HAVE YOU BEEN TO THE ALTAR LATELY?

Whatever they imagine, they will be able to do. So what is your excuse? Why aren't you dreaming?

Stop looking at the map of the United States and seeing blue and red. Start seeing the glory of the Lord hovering over our nation. The angels are ready for those who are not lukewarm, who hear what the Spirit is saying. The seraphim and cherubim are waiting. There are fire and sapphire stones. God is sitting in heaven and laughing because His enemies are coming to nothing, and this is all happening right now. That same coal that touched Isaiah on the altar is there among those burning coals right now.

PRAYER

Father, thank you so much for giving us this powerful insight into your throne room. You are so holy, and we are thankful that you have invited us to be with you at your altar in pure holiness. We receive the impartation in the name of Jesus. Amen!

What did the Holy Spirit reveal to you regarding this chapter?

_____

_____

_____

_____

_____

_____

_____

_____

_____

_____

_____

_____

_____

_____

_____

_____

_____

_____

_____

_____

_____

_____

_____

HAVE YOU BEEN TO THE ALTAR LATELY?

Everyone Will Give an Account

6

Therefore, each one must answer for himself
and give a personal account
of his own life before God.
—Romans 14:12 TPT

I celebrate Christmas starting on October 31 because the devil picked a fight with me, so I begin Christmas then. We put the tree up during *his* holiday, and Kathi and I start Christmas on Hallelujah Day, October 31, and we have

Christmas decorations at our house and share the celebration with friends.

You know the story of *How the Grinch Stole Christmas*. The Grinch is up on the hill with his dog, and he is saying that he will not let them have Christmas this year in Whoville. What can he do? His dog is afraid of him because he knows he will have to get dressed up as a reindeer to steal Christmas. Just like that Grinch, some entities right now are saying, "No matter what we do, they will still gather together and sing, and they are happy in Whoville." Even after the Grinch stole all their Christmas gifts, the Whos still came to the middle of town, held hands, and sang together in an unknown tongue.

Whether or not you believe it, some entities right now are set against you, and they are bent on stealing, killing, and destroying. I do not let that rule my life because we still have a chance to save people from hell.

Stop looking at blue and red, and start looking at God's heart for this nation. From the beginning, God gave us this nation so that we could have religious freedom. I am not getting political, but I am going back to my roots. I am going back to Bethel, and an altar is there. An altar is in this nation on the Mayflower, where forty-one people signed a compact and gave this nation over to God for religious freedom. Read the compact that is actually a covenant. I am falling back on those words, and that is not being political. That is a covenant that you have with God.

God chose you to be wherever you are in your nation; He chose you to be at that exact spot. I don't forget these things because I do not want to be like Jacob. I do not want to fall asleep and accidentally fall into what I should have known. Right now, angels are coming up and down, and traffic is going on in the heavenlies. A specific destiny and purpose has been chosen, not just for you but also for the state and the nation that you represent, wherever you are in the world. I am for you and for the covenant that God made with you and with your nation.

Fed Up with the Fake

Can you see the fakeness in everything? We were ministering in Switzerland, a neutral nation, so they don't get involved with other countries. Every day on our way to church to speak, we drove by the same building. One day, I asked what was inside. "Oh, they make ammo there," my friend said.

I could not help asking, "Wait a minute. You are disarmed, and you are a neutral country." I thought they were peaceful watchmakers. I continued, "So you are a neutral country, but it's okay to make ammo?"

He said, "Oh, we ship it out to other nations."

At what point do you all get bought out? Don't you see through all this, and don't you just get fed up with it? Don't you sometimes want to yell, "Shut up and stop being fake?" *You* can make a difference, but you have to feed yourself the Word of God. Then you have to go to the altar and get ignited. You can have the Word of God, but do you have experiential knowledge? Do you have the Holy Spirit as your Helper and Comforter? Do you have what it takes in war to stand up like a prophet and speak God's intent when everything is going wrong? Can you stand? They kill those people in their generation but then celebrate them as heroes in the next.

Jesus said that they killed the prophets, but now they are their heroes. Any Jewish person will brag about Elijah, but Elijah said, "Lord, they have killed Your prophets, they have torn down Your altars, and I alone am left, and they are seeking my life." (See Romans 11:3.)

Jesus said, "But now you seek to kill Me, a Man who has told you the truth which I heard from God." (See John 8:40.) When Jesus asked why they wanted to kill Him, they answered, "For a good work we do not stone You, but for blasphemy, and because You, being Man, make Yourself God." (See John 10:33.) "'For which is easier, to say, "Your sins are forgiven you," or to say, "Arise and walk?" But that you may know that the Son of Man has power on earth to forgive sins'—then He said to the paralytic, 'Arise, take up your bed, and go to your house'" (Matthew 9:5–6).

Jesus was poking at them when He said this in Matthew because they thought people were sick because of their own sin or that they were born that way because of their parent's sin. At what point do you start to be the litigator or the lawyer? When do you start to tell them that what they are saying is not panning out? When do you say, "Look at your life, and you are criticizing me because I pray in tongues?" I trust God and believe that His angels are working behind the scenes in our justice system right now. I believe that the lawyers are receiving supernatural help. I can still believe that because the Grinch hasn't stolen Christmas yet. He is still up on the hill, talking to his dog.

What the Whos physically had or didn't have in Whoville was not what made them happy. Their belongings and their gifts didn't make them happy. They had each other, which made them happy. They came to the town center, held hands, and sang their song.

HAVE YOU BEEN TO THE ALTAR LATELY?

Learning to Eat Your Manna Alone

You are going to have to have your altar experience. You must have your personal encounter with God because no one will do it for you.

The enemy never discerned what Jesus did, or he would have never crucified Him, but it was puzzling that they fell right into the trap. The enemy is confused right now because we are not affected. The enemy wonders why we aren't spending our days cowering in a corner because we lost. The demons wonder why we are still going out two by two to church or a conference. Why would you do this? All those things don't matter. What matters is that the body of Christ is getting together with other believers, hearing the Word of God, and being changed.

You have to have your altar experience, your personal encounter with God, because no one will do it for you. Everything is lukewarm right now. You will not get this intimacy with Jesus unless you go to the altar yourself. Jesus said to them, "I have food to eat of which you do not know." (See John 4:32.) He was trying to show them that He was feeding Himself by the very words that came from God. Jesus was a self-feeder and went to the mountains alone and ate every word that came from the mouth of God; it was what He lived on, and He told the devil that. (See Matthew 4:4.)

HAVE YOU BEEN TO THE ALTAR LATELY?

Jesus said to me, "Kevin, when I was in the desert, I had to stay there as a Son of Man, not the Son of God. The plan of satan was to get me to act as the Son of God."

The tempter said, "If You are the Son of God, command that these stones become bread." (See Matthew 4:3.) Jesus could not do that because He came to be in our shoes to be the perfect sacrifice for man. So if He did anything as the Son of God, it would disqualify what He was doing. That is what Jesus told me.

We have been dealing with people in our government who have been corrupt for years. They are so boastful and proud, and they have no idea that they will have to give an account one day. Everyone will have to give an account. You have to remember this: Every demon spirit that harasses you will one day be tormented for what they did to you, and they will be punished. Every person who does not repent will have to give an account, and they will find that they were not coming against you; they were coming against God.

What happened with Saul, who became Paul? (See Acts 9:4.) Jesus said, "Saul, Saul, why are you persecuting Me?"

Saul thought, *When did I persecute Jesus*? But Jesus equated Saul's persecution of Christians with persecution of Jesus Himself. It was a real eye-opening experience for Saul, who became Paul, and he realized then that he was fighting against God.

Jesus said to His disciples that a day is coming when people will kill you because they think they are doing God a favor. That was what Saul was doing. He thought he was doing the work of God by getting rid of these Christians. Saul, who became Paul, turned to the Lord, and you can now enjoy his letters. But remember, he was working against God and killing Christians at one time. God let it happen, not because He could not stop it, but because payday was coming.

PRAYER

Father, thank you so much for receiving your Word, and may everything that was of you take root and bring forth a harvest. I thank you, Father, for fruit that lasts. Lord, let them encounter the altar. I know, Lord, that they will never go back, and I believe that they will be permanently changed forever.

What did the Holy Spirit reveal to you regarding this chapter?

_____

_____

_____

_____

_____

_____

_____

_____

_____

_____

_____

_____

_____

_____

_____

_____

_____

_____

_____

_____

_____

Salvation Prayer

Lord God,

I confess that I am a sinner. I confess that I need your Son, Jesus. Please forgive me in His name.

Lord Jesus, I believe you died for me and that you are alive and listening to me now.

I now turn from my sins and welcome you into my heart. Come and take control of my life. Make me the kind of person you want me to be.

Now, fill me with your Holy Spirit, who will show me how to live for you. I acknowledge you before men as my Savior and my Lord.

In Jesus's name. Amen.

If you prayed this prayer, please contact us at: info@kevinzadai.com for more information and material. Go to www.kevinzadai.com for other exciting ministry materials.

Kevinzadai.com
Go to Warrior Notes TV for exclusive
ministry programming:
www.warriornotes.tv. To enroll in our
ministry school, go to:
www.warriornotesschool.com.

About Dr. Kevin Zadai

Kevin Zadai was called to ministry at the age of ten. He attended Central Bible College in Springfield, Missouri, where he received a bachelor of arts in theology. Later, he received missions' training at Rhema Bible College and a ThD at Primus University. He is currently ordained through Rev. Dr. Jesse and Rev. Dr. Cathy Duplantis. At age thirty-one, during a routine surgery, he found himself on the "other side of the veil" with Jesus. For forty-five minutes, the Master revealed spiritual truths and assigned him to a supernatural ministry. Kevin holds a commercial pilot license and has worked for Southwest Airlines for twenty-nine years as a flight attendant. He and his lovely wife, Kathi, reside in New Orleans, Louisiana.

HAVE YOU BEEN TO THE ALTAR LATELY?

Made in the USA
Columbia, SC
18 July 2021

42029571R00048